To/

VINTAGE
BORN IN 1974

Happy 50th Birthday

Take a trip back in time and discover everything you loved and maybe forgot about the 1970s.

Lots of love,

70s Child

Having been born in 1974, you witnessed the birth of new technologies that would change the world forever. You remember a world before technology invaded the everyday, unlike children born after the 90s. Having lived through a true childhood, you were able to play in the streets with your friends and make up games based on your imagination. There were many families who enjoyed a better standard of living than previous generations despite the social and economic unrest that characterized the decade. Consumerism grew as a result of families having more money to spend on leisure activities and products. There was a change in the fabric of society. Music and fashion are two of the most prominent examples of the move towards individualism. Amazing musicians and bands emerged during the 70s. The expansion of subcultures in society was accompanied by an explosion of new fashion styles. As a result of the divorce act passed in the late 1960s, the family structure began to change. One in eight families will be headed by a single parent by the end of the decade. Women's liberation is slowly gaining momentum. There is a growing number of women who stay in the workplace after getting married and having children. In society, there is a call for equality. Even so, when looking at advertising, it's clear that this was not achieved but rather was the seed of something greater. Taking a trip back to your childhood, this book revisits all those things you loved and knew as a child of the 70s.

50 YEARS AGO BACK IN 1974

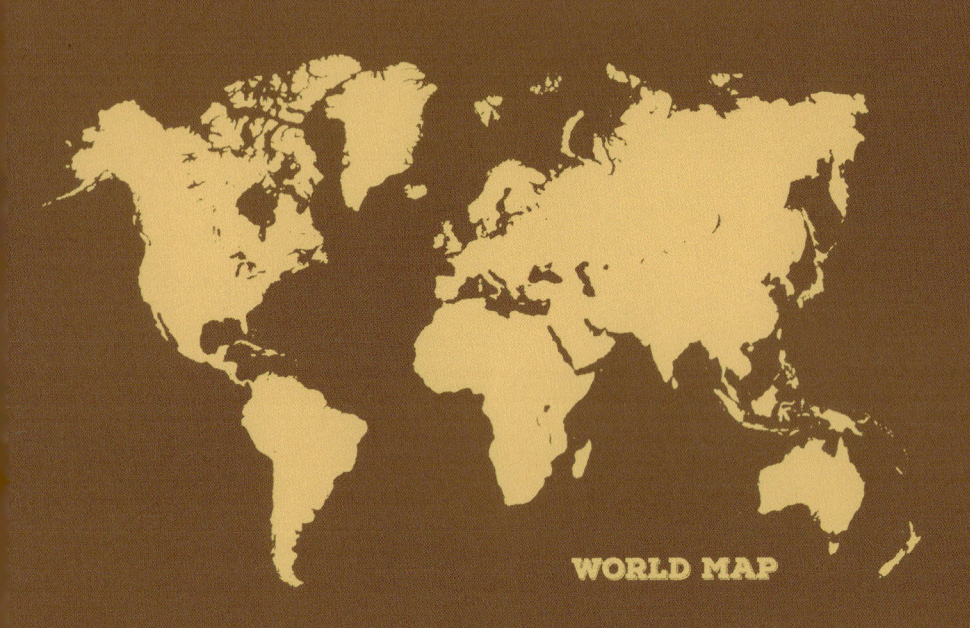

WORLD MAP

World Population
3.9 BILLION
Britain population
56.2 MILLION

2024
World Population
8.1 BILLION
Britain population
67.9 MILLION

MAJOR WORLD LEADERS

UK- PRIME MINISTER - EDWARD HEATH TILL 4 MARCH, JAMES HAROLD WILSON

US PRESIDENT - RICHARD NIXON TILL AUGUST 9 GERALD FORD

RUSSIA/SOVIET UNION - FIRST SECRETARY OF THE CPSU LEONID BREZHNEV

SOUTH AFRICA - PRIME MINISTER - BALTHAZAR JOHANNES VORSTER

ITALY - PRIME MINISTER - GIULIO ANDREOTTI

WEST GERMANY - CHANCELLOR - WILLY BRANDT

EAST GERMANY - ERICH HONECKER, CHAIRMAN OF THE COUNCIL OF STATE OF EAST GERMANY

FRANCE - PRESIDENT GEORGES POMPIDOU

CANADA - PRIME MINISTER - PIERRE TRUDEAU

CHINA - HEAD OF STATE - CHAIRMAN OF THE PEOPLE'S REPUBLIC OF CHINA DONG BIWU

PRESIDENT OF MEXICO PRESIDENT - LUIS ECHEVERRÍA

You Have Been Loved for

50 YEARS

Thats 600 months

2609 weeks   **18,262 days**

438,291 hrs

26,297,460 MINUTES

1,576,800,000 seconds

and counting...

Cost of living 1974

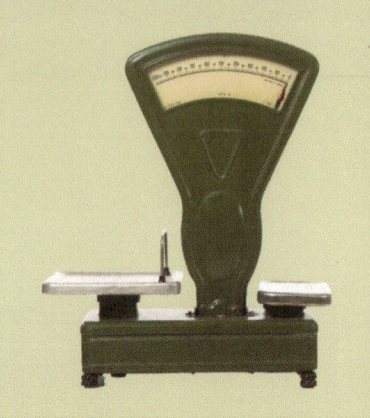

Average House £8915
In today's money that's approx £116,440

Average Salary £1,809
In today's money that's approx £23,500

Average Car price £1,600
In today's money that's approx £20,900

Gallon of petrol £0.53
In today's money that's approx £6.92

A dozen eggs £0.25	£3.90 in today's money
Loaf of Bread £0.10	£1.56 in today's money
2lb Sugar £0.10	£1.56 in today's money
12oz Kellogs cornflakes £0.11	£1.72 in today's money
1pt Milk £0.05	£0.78 in today's money
400g Bacon £0.34	£5.31 in today's money
Stork margarine 6 1/2p	£1.01 in today's money
8oz Nescafe coffee £0.47	£7.34 in today's money
Daily Mirror Newspaper 2.5 – 3p	£0.43 in today's money

Did You Know?

The first commercially produced Skittles were produced in 1974 by a British company. Jack Candies Ltd, a Mars distribution subsidiary, owns the copyright for an animated television advertisement from that year bearing the Galaxy logo. As an import confectionery, they were first introduced to North America in 1979. The United States began producing Skittles in 1982. Skittles gets its name from the sports game of the same name for its resemblance to items used in the game. D'Arcy Masius Benton & Bowles, an advertising agency in New York, created Skittles' "taste the rainbow" theme.

FIFA World Cup - Football enthusiasts around the world were disappointed by the absence of a FIFA World Cup in 1974. Political reasons caused this hiatus, disrupting the usual excitement and anticipation surrounding the event. It left a void in the football community, with fans eagerly anticipating 1978's World Cup.

Invention of the Rubik's Cube - In 1974, Rubik's Cube revolutionized the puzzle world. It quickly captured the imagination of people worldwide, becoming a sensation. Various competitions were organized to solve its intricate design, attracting enthusiasts who thrived on its conundrum-like nature.

Dungeons and Dragons debuts in January 1974 - Gary Gygax, Dave Arneson, and Don Kaye developed Dungeons & Dragons, the iconic fantasy role-playing game. Based on miniature wargaming and J.R.R. Tolkien's Lord of the Rings, the game was published by their own company, Tactical Studies Rules. Globally, D&D has served as a creative social outlet for over four decades.

Top Ten Baby Names

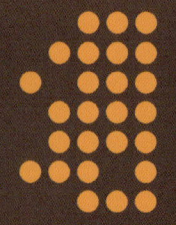

- SARAH
- CLAIRE
- NICOLA
- EMMA
- LISA
- JOANNE
- MICHELLE
- HELEN
- SAMANTHA
- KAREN

- PAUL
- MARK
- DAVID
- ANDREW
- RICHARD
- CHRISTOPHER
- JAMES
- SIMON
- MICHAEL
- MATTHEW

50 & famous

- **OLICVIA COLEMAN** 30TH JANUARY
- **CHRISTIAN BALE** 30TH JANUARY
- **LEONARDO DICAPRIO** NOVEMBER 11TH
- **ALANIS MORISSETTE** JUNE 1ST
- **JIMMY FALLON** SEPTEMBER 19TH
- **VICTORIA BECKHAM** APRIL 17TH
- **PENELOPE CRUZ** 30TH APRIL
- **ELIZABETH BANKS** 10TH FEBRUARY
- **JOAQUIN PHOENIX**
- **KATE MOSS** 16TH JANUARY
- **ROBBIE WILLIAMS** 13TH FEBRUARY
- **EVA MENDES** 5TH MARCH

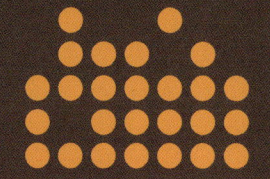

Music

Whenever you think of the 70s, you can't help but think of Glam Rock. Glam Rock provided an oasis of sparkle in an otherwise dreary, depressing political, social, and economic landscape. Elton John, David Bowie, and T-Rex are some of the icons of Glam music. There was an abundance of colour, style, and personality in the music of the 70s. Punk was also born during this revolt against the 'norm'. Sex Pistols, arguably the most well-known example of this, came later on in the 70s. The British music scene was awash with loud, diverse music scenes that refused to fade into the background.

1970 Edison Lighthouse
1971 T Rex
1972 The New Seekers
1973 Slade
1974 Abba
1975 David Bowie
1976 Abba
1977 Donna Summer
1978 Boomtown Rats

TOP POP HITS 1974

For the first two weeks of 1974, Slade's 1973 Christmas hit "Merry Xmas Everybody" remained at number-one. The New Seekers featuring Lyn Paul had the first number-one single of the year with "You Won't Find Another Fool Like Me.".

There were 21 number-one singles in 1974, with Mud having the most hits. Mud's "Tiger Feet" song spent seven weeks in the top 10 (including four weeks at number one) and was certified gold by the BPI.

Three other top 10 hits were also produced by the glam-rock group this year, including the year's Christmas number-one single, "Lonely This Christmas".

Terry Jacks' "Seasons In The Sun" topped the UK charts for four weeks this year, becoming the second best-selling single of the year.

A three-week stint at number-one in March was Paper Lace's third best-selling song in 1974, "Billy Don't Be A Hero".

The Three Degrees scored the fourth best-selling track of the year with "When Will I See You Again", which topped the charts for two weeks in August.

The top ten best-selling singles of the year also included singles by David Essex, Charles Aznavour, Carl Douglas, Ken Boothe, and The Rubettes.

Sir Roderick David Stewart CBE

Rod Stewart is one of the best-selling music artists of all time, having sold over 250 million records worldwide.
- 10 No.1 albums
- 31 top ten single hits
- 6 No.1 hits

He was knighted in the 2016 Birthday Honours for services to music and charity.

Marc Bolan; born Mark Feld; 30) died 1977

Marc had many strings to his bow but was most famously Lead singer of the band T.Rex and was one of the pioneers of glam rock.

The Supremes split in 1970, Ross then went from success to success spanning; a solo music career, television, film and stage performances. Ross' released her debut solo album that same year. Everything Is Everything, gave her, her first UK number-one single "I'm Still Waiting".

She then dominated the world with her spectacular globe trotting sell out concert tours.

Albums - she enjoyed hit after hit with Touch Me in the Morning (1973), Mahogany (1975) and Diana Ross (1976) and their number-one hit singles, "Touch Me in the Morning", "Theme from Mahogany" and "Love Hangover", respectively. Ross further released numerous top-ten hits Throughout the 70s and into the decades that followed.

British rock group Mungo Jerry enjoyed success in the early 1970s, The group's name was inspired by the poem "Mungojerrie and Rumpleteazer", by T.S Elliot

Their biggest and most widely known hit was "In the Summertime".

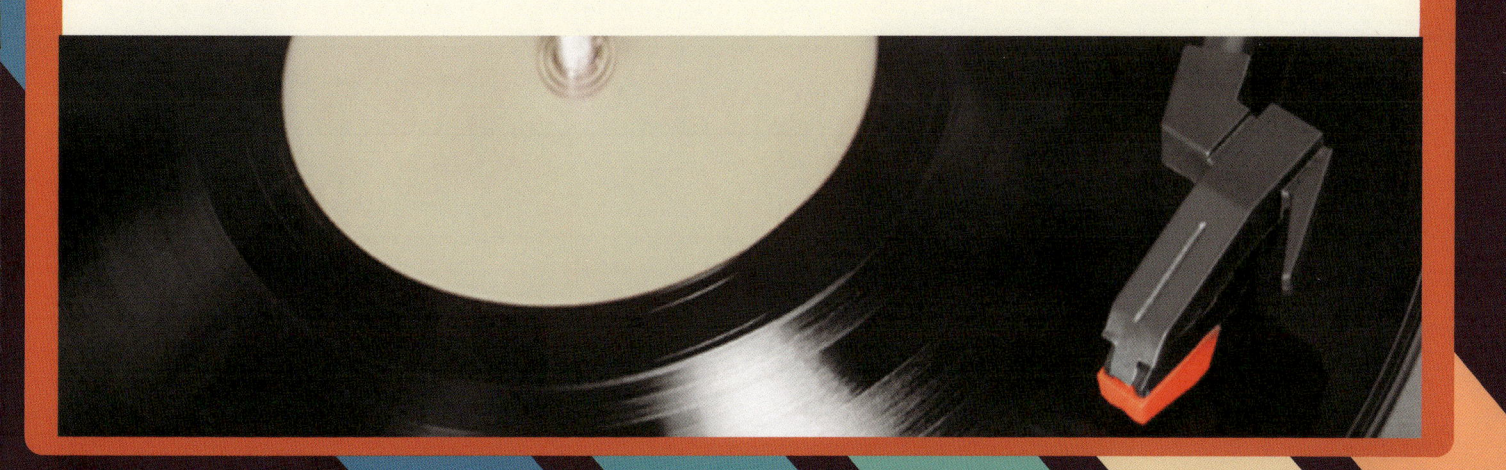

TRANSPORT

The first Pan Am Boeing jet landed at Heathrow in 1970, kicking off the era of commercial flights. It was with that first flight that flying became more accessible to 'ordinary' families. All of a sudden, travel around the world became a realistic possibility, something most people couldn't imagine. Before this, British holidays were very much seaside trips or Butlins resorts if you were lucky. Changing technology influenced almost every aspect of life in the 1970s. The Concorde passenger aircraft, which is the fastest passenger aircraft in the world, was one of the most spectacular technological achievements of the 21st century. A real engineering feat, Concorde was built by Britain & France and first flew in 1976. At a speed of 2,100 kilometers per hour. 1976 to 2003 was the lifespan of Concorde. The airline's retirement was partly due to its extremely high fares, which were unaffordable for most people. Concorde flights between London and Washington originally cost £431 each. The number of cars on the road today is estimated to be 39 million. That number was closer to 13 million in 1971 or just a third of what it is today. Despite this, infrastructure growth has not kept pace. There were 246,700 miles of road in total in 2018, up less than a quarter from 203,400 miles in 1971.

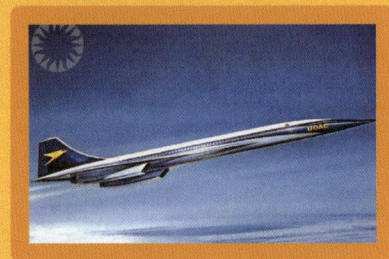

At the turn of the decade, the top four car manufacturers all released brand-new models. Ford Escort, which was launched in 1967, was one of the newer versions. As well as the Ford Capri, which is credited with bringing sports cars into the mainstream.

Top ten selling cars of the 70s

1. Ford Cortina
2. Ford Escort
3. Mini
4. Morris Marina
5. Vauxhall Viva
6. Austin/Morris 1100/1300
7. Austin Allegro
8. Ford Capri
9. Hillman Avenger
10. Austin Maxi

CHANGING TRENDS

Walking to work was the most common form of transportation between the 1890s and the 1930s and remained the main means of commuting for one-third to one-fifth of the population in small towns and cities as late as the 1970s. Bicycle use declined after 1950 as other forms of transportation became available. The decline continued until the mid-1970s when it levelled off, and usage has remained fairly consistent since then.

FORD ESCORT

CAPRI
From your Mercury deal

ist : $8.50 (each kit) Plus tax
List : $7.80 (each kit) Plus tax
List : $26.00 each. Plus tax
e your Ford Dealer for these new accessory releases
Ford

BRITISH LEYLAND build a car to suit your requirements. Check the model specification chart at the front of this booklet and see which car most nearly fits your own individual needs.
For further details of any of the models illustrated in this booklet, please write direct to the manufacturer whose address is given below.
ADVERTISING DEPARTMENT BRITISH LEYLAND (AUSTIN MORRIS) LIMITED LONGBRIDGE, BIRMINGHAM (Austin, Morris, MG, Wolseley)
PUBLICITY DEPARTMENT JAGUAR CARS LIMITED BROWNS LANE, ALLESLEY COVENTRY CV5 9DR (Jaguar, Daimler)
SALES DEPARTMENT THE ROVER COMPANY LIMITED SOLIHULL, WARWICKSHIRE (Rover, Land-Rover, Range Rover)
PUBLICITY DEPARTMENT TRIUMPH MOTOR COMPANY LIMITED FLETCHAMSTEAD HIGHWAY CANLEY, COVENTRY CV4 9DB (Triumph)
BRITISH LEYLAND ALSO PRODUCE A COMPLETE RANGE OF TRUCKS, BUSES, AUTOMOTIVE COMPONENTS, EARTHWORK AND CONSTRUCTION EQUIPMENT.
Information can be obtained from the addresses below.
Truck and Bus Division British Leyland Motor Corporation Leyland, Preston PR5 1SN
Special Products Division British Leyland Motor Corporation Invicta Works, Grantham Lincolnshire.
AUSTIN·DAIMLER·JAGUAR·MG·MINI·MORRIS·ROVER·TRIUMPH·WOLSELEY

Films

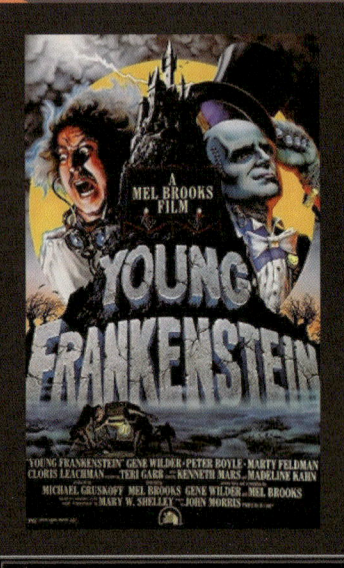

Young Frankenstein

The elaborate electrical machinery for Frankenstein (1931) and its sequels was designed by Ken Strickfaden, who was still alive and living in Los Angeles at the time Mel Brooks was planning this movie. In Brooks' visit to Strickfaden, he found that all the equipment had been stored in the garage. In exchange for renting the equipment, Brooks gave Strickfaden the screen credit he hadn't received for the original films.

The Godfather Part II

Roth's shirt changes during his birthday party. As a result of weather problems, the two-minute scene took over a week to shoot, and the original shirt was lost during the process. By drawing an approximation of the pattern onto a plain shirt, the production designer attempted to recreate it, but it didn't quite match.

Earthquake

A bizarre coincidence occurred on the first day of shooting, when the area was rocked by an earthquake. Even more bizarrely, an earthquake also struck at the location where the last day of shooting took place.

Films 1974

- **THE STING (WON BEST MOTION PICTURE OSCAR)**
- **THE EXORCIST**
- **THE MAN WITH THE GOLDEN GUN**
- **ENTER THE DRAGON**
- **THE THREE MUSKETEERS**
- **PAPILLON**
- **ROBIN HOOD**
- **THE GREAT GATSBY**
- **THE TOWERING INFERNO**
- **GOLDEN VOYAGE OF SINBAD**
- **BLAZING SADDLES**
- **CONFESSIONS OF A WINDOW CLEANER**
- **STARDUST**
- **LAST TANGO IN PARIS**
- **AMERICAN GRAFFITI**

Popular 70s TV Shows

In 1971, 91% of families owned a television

The early 1970s were characterised by a focus on comedy shows. Except for BBC's Steptoe and Son, ITV dominated this market. A great deal of progress was being made by the BBC toward assuming the comedy role by the mid-70s. 'The Good Life' (1975) and 'Faulty Towers' (1975) remain popular today. In the 70s, the BBC overtook ITV in producing the best and most popular shows on TV. Although you may have been too young to watch these shows at the time of their release, you will probably recognise some of those films. Today, many of these are still airing as repeats on television. Do you know what the big news of the decade is? Colour TV is available! Colour broadcasting began on 3 of the main stations by the end of the 1960s.

ARE YOU BEING SERVED?
UK (BBC) Situation Comedy. BBC 1 1973-9; 1981; 1983; 1985
ANTIQUES ROADSHOW
UK (BBC) Antiques. BBC 1 1979–
ALL CREATURES GREAT AND SMALL
UK (BBC) Drama. BBC 1 1978-80; 1983; 1985;1988-90
THE BENNY HILL SHOW
UK (BBC) Comedy. BBC 1 1955-1968; Thames 1969-89
BLAKE'S 7
UK (BBC) Science Fiction. BBC 1 1978-81
BLESS THIS HOUSE
UK (Thames) Situation Comedy. ITV 1971-4, 1976
CALLAN
UK (ABC/Thames) Secret Agent Drama. ITV 967-72
CILLA
UK (BBC) Variety. BBC 1
CORONATION STREET
UK (Granada) Drama. ITV 1960- present day
CROSSROADS
UK (ATV/Central/Carlton) Drama. ITV 1964-88; ITV 1 2001-3
DAD'S ARMY
UK (BBC) Situation Comedy. BBC 1 1968-77
DOCTOR WHO
UK (BBC) Science Fiction. BBC 1 1963-89
THE DES O'CONNOR SHOW
UK (ATV) Comedy.
FAWLTY TOWERS
UK (BBC). Situation Comedy. BBC 2 1975; 1979
THE GENERATION GAME
UK (BBC) Game Show. BBC 1 1971-82; 1990- 2002
GEORGE AND MILDRED
UK (Thames) Situation Comedy. ITV 1976-9
THE GOOD LIFE
UK (BBC), Situation Comedy. BBC 1 1975-8
GRANGE HILL
UK (BBC/Mersey), Children's Drama. BBC 1978-
LAST OF THE SUMMER WINE
UK (BBC) Situation Comedy. BBC 1 1973; 1975-6; 1978-9; 1981-93; 1995–
PLEASE SIR!
UK (LWT) Situation Comedy. ITV 1968-72
MORCAMBE AND WISE
UK (ATV) Comedy. 1961-7; BBC 1 1968-76; ITV 978-84
MONTY PYTHON'S FLYING CIRCUS
UK (BBC) Comedy. BBC 1 1969-73; BBC 2 1973
OPPORTUNITY KNOCKS
UK (Associated Rediffusion/ABC/Thames/BBC) Talent Show. ITV 1956-78; BBC 1 1987-90
PRISONER: CELL BLOCK H
Australia (Grundy) Drama. ITV 1979-87
SOME MOTHERS DO 'AVE 'EM
UK (BBC) Situation Comedy. BBC 1 1973-5; 1978
STEPTOE AND SON
UK (BBC) Situation Comedy. BBC 1 1962-5; 1970; 1972-4
THE SWEENEY
UK (Euston Films/Thames) Police Drama. ITV 975-6; 1978
THIS IS YOUR LIFE
UK (BBC/Thames) Entertainment. BBC

Adverts in the 70s

More houses than ever owned a colour TV with multiple channels during the 1970s. As a result, people had more choices than they had ever had before. This changed the way products were marketed, and brands were quick to take advantage of this new opportunity. Traditional advertising was done primarily in newspapers and magazines, but more brands were turning to television. It led to a consumer-based approach rather than the existing product-centric approach, giving consumers more control - if they didn't like the advertising they saw they switched over.

Although advertisements were still largely product-focused at the beginning of the decade, brands started digging deep into the narrative of why people should buy their brand over others as they recognised the importance of appealing to customers and communicating the reasons why their product was superior. Today, comparison ads are still seen in advertising as a result of this. A couple of obvious examples are Burger King versus McDonald's, and Pepsi versus Coke. Mothercare's advertisement on the following page shows another early example "See how much more your money buys at Mothercare..." showing not just the product benefits but how they compare to other brands. There were more rules & regulations in the 70s advertising world than in previous decades. Products no longer had the same elastic approach to listing their benefits. Regulations allowed for a more honest approach, which in turn increased consumer confidence. As you can see on the following page, PLJ lemon juice regulations weren't quite as strict as they are now. In short, this miracle juice will help you lose weight, look gorgeous, and have glowing skin. With the advancement of technology, companies were able to collect more information about their customers. For the first time, companies were gathering data to target their advertising. This included demographic information, analysis of consumer spending behaviour, and projections based on analysis of previous data. These were used in campaigns to increase demand for the brand/product. Ads are also increasingly emphasising emotional approaches. The result was advertisements we would now find offensive and would certainly not see on our televisions. A major culprit is sexual innuendo, a sign of how different cultures were just five decades ago.

Food brands and soap powder brands dominated TV ads in the 70s. The following double page features original 1970s ads. You might also remember the Smash Martians? Katie, who had appeared in OXO advertisements since the 1950s, travelled to America to tell her American friends about this wonderful cooking aid. As a result, the brand gained a sense of glamour. Originally made in 1903, HP Fruity Sauce is the original HP sauce. To offer a milder alternative to the original sauce, fruity sauce was developed in 1969. Are you aware that HP stands for Houses of Parliament? Frederick Gibson Garter, a Nottingham grocer, invented the original recipe. In order to settle a debt with Edwin Samson Moore of the Midlands vinegar company, he sold the recipe for £150.

Ad for Coffee Mate in a 1972 magazine. The product developed in 1961 was particularly popular throughout the 70s.

Joules Bel founded Babybel in 1865. With over 2 billion units sold worldwide, this long-established brand continues to be a success today

Ceylon tea and PG Tips- it wasn't until the 1970's that tea companies began selling tea bags instead of loose leaf tea. Although teabags were sold earlier in the century, they didn't catch on until the 1970s. This change in consumption was driven by advertising.

Old Spice's Christmas advertisement shows various gift sets. Your dad probably received a few of these along with some patterned socks during the 70's.

Vencat Curry Powder - curry was not popular before the 1970s. Due to the fact that most housewives were unfamiliar with the ingredient, the original ads provided recipe suggestions.

Hoover Gas fire, The Show-off- 1970 advert. The gas fire has been in households since the 1940s, but due to post-war austerity it was not commonplace until the 1960s, and even then it was used sparingly. With advertising, gas fires became increasingly popular in the 1970s as real coal fires became obsolete.

Wright's coal tar soap has been one of the most popular soaps in many homes since the 1860s. Even today, the soap can be used to treat various skin disorders.

Here's where natural beauty counts
'Tea bags? The Mothers' Union would never agree.'
BROOKE BOND PG TIPS
The Dunlop family adds colour to comfort.
Dunlop Bright ideas for keeping your feet snug.
Out and about
Late-night line-up
mothercare shops
It's here! New HP Fruity
the sister sauce to the great HP
HP FRUITY SAUCE
More than just a pretty face
H. SAMUEL
CRIMPLENE
DOUBLE JERSEY
60"/62" wide
from 29/11 PER YARD Inc. P/Tax
AUTUMN 1970
Wonderful–uncrushable designs for every occasion. Wonderful co-ordinating colourways exclusive to us. Send now for free samples and open up a new world for yourself in CRIMPLENE.
FULLY GUARANTEED.
KENROSS FABRICS LTD. (Dept. WH1), P.O. Box 162, Beaumont Leys Lane, Leicester
CEYLON
36 TEA BAGS
GOLD CROWN
36 TEA BAGS
Brewhurst
36 tea bags
(113G) 4oz net 2/11
The flavour test you can make with your eyes.
Ceylon puts the flavour in tea bags

From the generous pastures of France. A soft hearted cheese to melt the stout hearted British.
FULL FAT SOFT
BABYBEL
CHEESE
With Coffee-mate every cup of coffee tastes like coffee made with cream
Coffee-mate.
It's the only thing for coffee only
The Golden Cube guide to herbs and spices.
OXO
VENCAT
Curry Powder
makes the difference!
Chicken, beef or lamb all discover an exciting new flavour with Vencat curry powder made from genuine Indian spices. Vencat has the secret that can turn a simple dish into a sensation.
VENCAT
CURRY POWDER
DON'T JUST COOK IT — CURRY IT.
Who wants to come up smelling like a rose?
Wright's
Old Spice have a gift for pleasing all the men in your life.
Old Spice
Merry Christmas and a Happy Old Spice.
SHULTON
show-off
Hoover Highlight gas fire
HOOVER

Fashion 1970s

As the swinging Sixties gave way to the 1970s, fashion had become more accessible. There were multiple movements of the era reflected in the boutiques' individual styles. As new technologies emerged, the fashion industry was heavily impacted. It was mainly influenced by the availability of cheap fabrics through mass production. Polyester was embraced with wild abandon during the 70s, referred to as the 'Polyester decade'. At the time, it didn't seem to bother anyone that it was cheap and didn't allow any air to pass through. For both men and women, tight-fitted tops and wide bell-bottom trousers were typical silhouettes of the 70s. The family photo album may contain some spectacular flares with platform shoes!

It was the 1970s that saw a move toward individualism. There was a move away from the community spirit prevalent in the 1960s. Fashion influenced music, and music influenced fashion, allowing individuals to experiment with non-conformist styles. In mainstream society, we can see the beginnings of a much more casual approach to fashion. Are you familiar with the Peacock revolution? Although you would not have been old enough to participate, perhaps an older sibling or family member strutted around town in ruffled lacy shirts with lace on the cuffs and neckline. A sight to behold, hence the name Peacock Revolution.

Designer Eyewear

1970s Fashion

Images were taken from an advertisement for Marks & Spencers in Woman & Home from the 1970s. The article examines the dilemma of what to wear at work now that more and more women continue to work after marriage. Women's trouser suits grew in popularity throughout the 1970s.

As with adult fashion, children's wear followed bright colours, patterns, and stripes, as well as knitwear and crochet. The adverts illustrated that fashion styles were still influenced by the 1960s and further back to the 1930s and 1940s. Modern fashion styles incorporate details from the past with innovations in fabrics.

70s Toys

As a child of the '70s, you probably remember classics like Chopper bikes, roller skates, space hoppers, and the Atari computer. Let's reminisce about other 70's toys that were very popular.

Sindy doll wins 1970 Toy of the Year. Toys are sold in supermarkets. The neon Nerf Ball (costing £1.25) was the must-have Christmas toy. Katie Kopycat was named the 1971 Toy of the Year. We also witnessed the arrival of the Spacehopper and the beginning of the Clackers craze. The Mastermind board game cost a whopping £1.64 and was ranked number one on Santa's toy list.

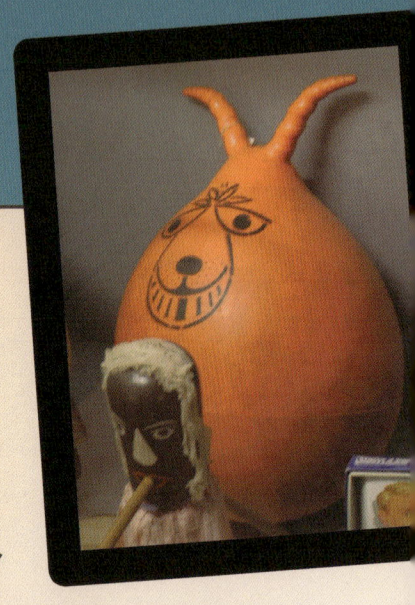

The 1972 Plasticraft modelling kit won the coveted Toy of the Year award. A feature in Toy Trader forecasts the growth of leisuredromes - theme park shopping centres. The Uno card game (costs £1.01) is a Christmas must-have.

The retail awards introduced a new category, game of the year, won by Invicta's Mastermind. Plastic is in short supply due to industrial & economic issues, which is a problem for toy manufacturers. On average, children receive 9p in pocket money. Chelsea Girl and Daisy are brand-new dolls this year. A Christmas must-have is Shrinky Dinks; large sheets of pre-painted shapes or colours that shrink in a hot oven.

In 1974, Lego won the Toy of the Year award for the first time. Trade is adversely affected by the 3-day week. Boxing toys Raving Bonkers, Denys Fisher Potter's Wheel, and the game Lexidata were among the biggest hits of the year. Fantasy tabletop role-playing game Dungeons & Dragons is a must-have for Christmas (costs £3.69).

1975 Lego wins again as Toy of the Year. The 40th anniversary of Monopoly is celebrated. Also celebrating a relatively young 25-year-old, Cluedo. Womblemania hits Britain. The theme tune might be familiar to you!

Game of Othello (costs £2.76) is a Christmas must-have.

In 1976, Peter Powell Kites won Toy of the Year as kites enjoyed a resurgence in popularity. Mattel set up shop in the UK 75 years after Meccano was invented. Streaker, a toy parodying yo-yos and hula hoops was the flop of the year. Christmas must-have toy - Magna Doodle (cost £2.63 - still available today).

The 1977 Toy of the Year award was given to Playpeople by Playmobil. This year's popular toys include slime, the Othello strategy board game, and Holly Hobbie. These Star Wars figurines cost £1.44 each and are a Christmas must-have.

The Combine Harvester made in Britain was the 1978 Toy of the Year. Huggy Bear is Chad Valley's first clinging bear. There is a new line of Star Wars toys on the market. Board and card games were launched by Omar Sharif at the NEC's Toy Fair. There were a number of big hits this year, such as Play-Doh Barber Shop - a childhood classic, Star Wars Force Beams, Matchbox Powertrack, and Mr. Men, as well as Skirrid, a new game that was a hit among adults and kids alike. Hungry Hippos (£3.94) was a Christmas must-have.

Do you remember?

Popular 70s Children's TV shows

In 1968, Elisabeth Beresford created a series of books featuring furry creatures called the Wombles. A BBC-commissioned children's television show helped boost the characters' national profile in the UK in the mid-1970s. Stop-motion animation was used to create the series, which became an instant hit. The UK was hit by Womblemania and a number of spin-off novelty songs charted.

BBC Bristol produced Animal Magic, a kid's television series from 1962 to 1983. The show first aired fortnightly, then weekly in 1964.

A series originally made in black & white in 1958, Ivor the Engine enjoyed a revival in 1975 when new programmes were created using colour television

Playaway with Brian Cant. Cant, Brian (12 July 1933 - 19 June 2017). The programmes Playaway (1971–84) were hosted or co-hosted by Cant. From birth to the teen years, you'll surely remember this!

Originally shown on BBC's Blue Peter, Bleep and Booster is a children's cartoon series by William Timym. Between 1964 and 1977, 313 five-minute episodes were released.

David McKee created Mr. Benn in 1971. Red Knight was the first episode.

The BBC aired Crackerjack from 14 September 1955 until 21 December 1984 (except during the year 1971). It was a popular variety show for kids that lasted for four decades and was enjoyed by several generations.

Stop-motion animation children's television series The Clangers (BBC1 1969-1972). A small moon-like planet is home to a family of mouse-like creatures. They converse in a strange whistle-like language and are sustained by green soup and blue string pudding.

Do you remember?

- **Tiswas**
- **Captain Pugwash**
- **Rainbow**
- **Basil Brush**
- **Trumpton Fire Brigade**
- **Roobarb & Custard**
- **Bagpuss** 13 episodes broadcast in 1974.
- **Banana Splits**

1974 UK Events

- 1st Jan - New Year's Day is celebrated as a public holiday for the first time.

- In response to the energy crisis, the UK starts working three days a week on January 6

- A protracted miners' strike prompted Edward Heath to call for a 'snap' general election on February 7

- 12 February – BBC1 first airs the children's television series Bagpuss, made by Peter Firmin and Oliver Postgate's Smallfilms in stop motion animation.

- 14th Feb- With a £350,000 move to Everton, Birmingham City forward Bob Latchford becomes Britain's most expensive footballer.

- Ian Ball fails in his attempt to kidnap HRH Princess Anne and Captain Mark Phillips outside Buckingham Palace on 20 March.

- After declaring a state of emergency, the government re-establishes direct rule over Northern Ireland.

- 6 April - Brighton hosts the 19th Eurovision Song Contest. ABBA wins the contest with their song "Waterloo", making them the first group to win. They later became internationally successful.

- First Division title for Leeds United won on 24 April.

- As a result of Kevin Keegan scoring twice and Steve Heighway scoring the other goal, Liverpool wins the FA Cup for the second time, defeating Newcastle United 3-0 in the Wembley final.

- In the final episode of Planet of the Spiders, Jon Pertwee leaves Doctor Who due to the death of Roger Delgado, a close acting friend.

- 24th June - There is a ritt within the Labour Party after the government admits to testing nuclear weapons in the United

- On July 17th, the IRA begins bombing mainland Britain and bomb The Tower of London, the Houses of Parliament, and Birmingham

- Ten thousand Greek Cypriots protest in London against the Turkish invasion of Cyprus on 21 July.
- Bessemer steel production in Britain ends on 28 July at Workington.
- On 18 September, Harold Wilson announces that the second general election will be held on 10 October.
- Ceefax is launched by the BBC on 23 September - one of the first public service information systems
- The University of Oxford admits women undergraduates to five previously all-male colleges.
- 7th November - Following his children's nanny's murder, Lord Lucan disappears.
- As of 13 November, McDonald's has opened its first UK location in Woolwich, South East London.
- 24 November – The Birmingham Six are charged with the Birmingham pub bombings.
- The Prevention of Terrorism Act is passed on 27 November.
- London premieres The Man with the Golden Gun, James Bond's ninth film. Roger Moore plays James Bond in the second of seven Bond films.
- The first episode of Roger Hargreaves' Mr. Men television series was broadcast on BBC1 on 31 December.
- The Chinese government donates two giant pandas to the British government, Ching-Ching and Chia-Chia.
- Mitsubishi makes its first imports to Britain under the Colt brand, bringing the number of Japanese automakers to five in the United Kingdom.

World Events

Alaska Oil pipeline
Alaska Oil pipeline construction begins

Richard Nixon becomes the first US president forced to resign

On August 9th, 1974, Richard Nixon resigns from office. During a televised address the previous day, he announced his resignation. As a result of his involvement in the Watergate Scandal, Nixon faced near-certain impeachment and conviction by the US Congress.

Nixon's involvement in illegal activities within his administration led to the Watergate Scandal, which began in 1972 at the beginning of his second term as US president. Nixon associates sabotage political opponents by breaking into Democratic party headquarters. Rather than facing a trial and being removed from office, Nixon resigned. Ford, Nixon's vice president, pardoned Nixon immediately after he took office.

Georges Pompidou
Georges Pompidou dies while in office as French president

26-year-old Stephen King published his debut novel, "Carrie," in April 1974.
King actually wrote four novels before he published "Carrie," the first to achieve commercial success. In the story, a bullied and sheltered teenage girl discovers that she has telekinetic powers, ultimately using them to seek revenge. There is no doubt that the novel revitalized the horror genre during the decade, as it became extremely popular. There was also an Academy Award-nominated film

The much anticipated boxing match between Muhammad Ali and George Foreman takes place in Kinshasa, Zaire.

Despite being considered one of the greatest boxers of all time, Muhammad Ali was stripped of his heavyweight title in 1967 for refusing to sign up for the Vietnam war draft. A lengthy ban from boxing was also imposed upon him.

In 1974, Muhammad Ali and George Foreman agreed to fight for the heavyweight title.

In the boxing match, Ali knocked out Foreman in the eighth round, becoming only the second former heavyweight champion to regain his title.

The Symbionese Liberation Army kidnaps Patricia Hearst

the 19-year-old daughter of publisher Randolph Hearst By the time she was found and arrested 19 months after being abducted, she had committed serious crimes with members of the group. Before trial, there was speculation that her family's resources would enable her to avoid prison time. Despite being sentenced to 35 years, she only served seven.

West Germany - FIFA World Cup

In July, West Germany won the FIFA World Cup. West Germany hosted the football tournament during the previous month. The Netherlands were defeated by the host country in the final. The third and fourth places went to Poland and Brazil, respectively. The 16 teams that qualified played 38 matches in total. In total, 97 goals were scored during the World Cup, which was attended by over 1.8 million people. For the first time, Australia, East Germany, Haiti, and Zaire (Democratic Republic of the Congo) qualified for the FIFA World Cup.

Charles de Gaulle Airport

A new airport opens in Paris, France, called Charles de Gaulle Airport.

Lucy an almost complete hominid skeleton

The skeleton of Lucy, an almost complete hominid from Africa, dates back over three million years.

The first hominid skeleton dating back to 3.2 million years ago was discovered by paleontologist Donald Johanson in Ethiopia on November 24, 1974. It was determined that the skeleton belonged to an early human ancestor species called Australopithecus afarensis, which was about forty percent complete. Upon discovering the skeleton, scientists named her Lucy. Lucy was the oldest known example of an ancestor of the human species. Lucy was likely a female, walked upright, measured about three and a half feet tall, and had ape-like facial features, based on the skeletal evidence. At the time, it was a huge scientific discovery.

World Wide Inflation

Fuel, food, and manufacturing costs rise dramatically as a result of worldwide inflation

70s Inventions

1972

Hamilton introduces the world's first electronic digital wristwatch. The retail price is $2,100, which is over $12K in today's dollars.

1971 Floppy Disk

The first floppies were created by IBM engineers working on a reliable way to load instructions and data onto mainframe computers. In 1971, IBM began selling floppies. It wasn't until 1972 that they received a patent, and then Apple released their Apple II with a 5-inch floppy disk that their success began. Consequently, the general public was able to load programs and data onto their home PCs easily.

Blakenbaker invented what is widely considered the first personal computer while working at Kenbar Corporation in 1970. Early in 1971, Kenbak-I was released.

Sony Walkman 1979

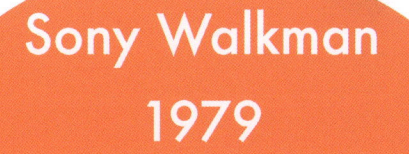

It was this invention that shaped the culture of the 1980s. It revolutionized the way young people listen to music. The Walkman became an instant hit in 1979. A mixed tape on a walkman was a joy for many teenagers during the 80s.

When Intel released the 4004 microprocessor in 1971, it was the world's first microprocessor.

US President Barack Obama awarded the National Medal of Technology and Innovation to Stanley Mazor, Federico Faggin, and Ted Holff, co-inventors of the microprocessor.

70s Inventions

Rubix Cube

Designed by Erno Rubik (architecture professor) to teach spatial relationships to his students. The toy became one of the most popular toys of the 1980s. The challenge continues to be popular today!

In 1977, 3M launched a "Press 'n Peel" bookmark in four cities, but the results were disappointing. When the rollout introduction began in 1979, 3M instead issued free samples and rebranded its product as "Post-Its," which began to be sold across the country on April 6, 1980.

Early in 1971, Busicom released the pocket-sized electronic calculator LE-120A "HANDY".

An engineer at Kodak invented the first self-contained digital camera in 1975. Black and white photographs were taken with the camera created by Steven Sasson, which weighed 8lbs.

Mobile phones

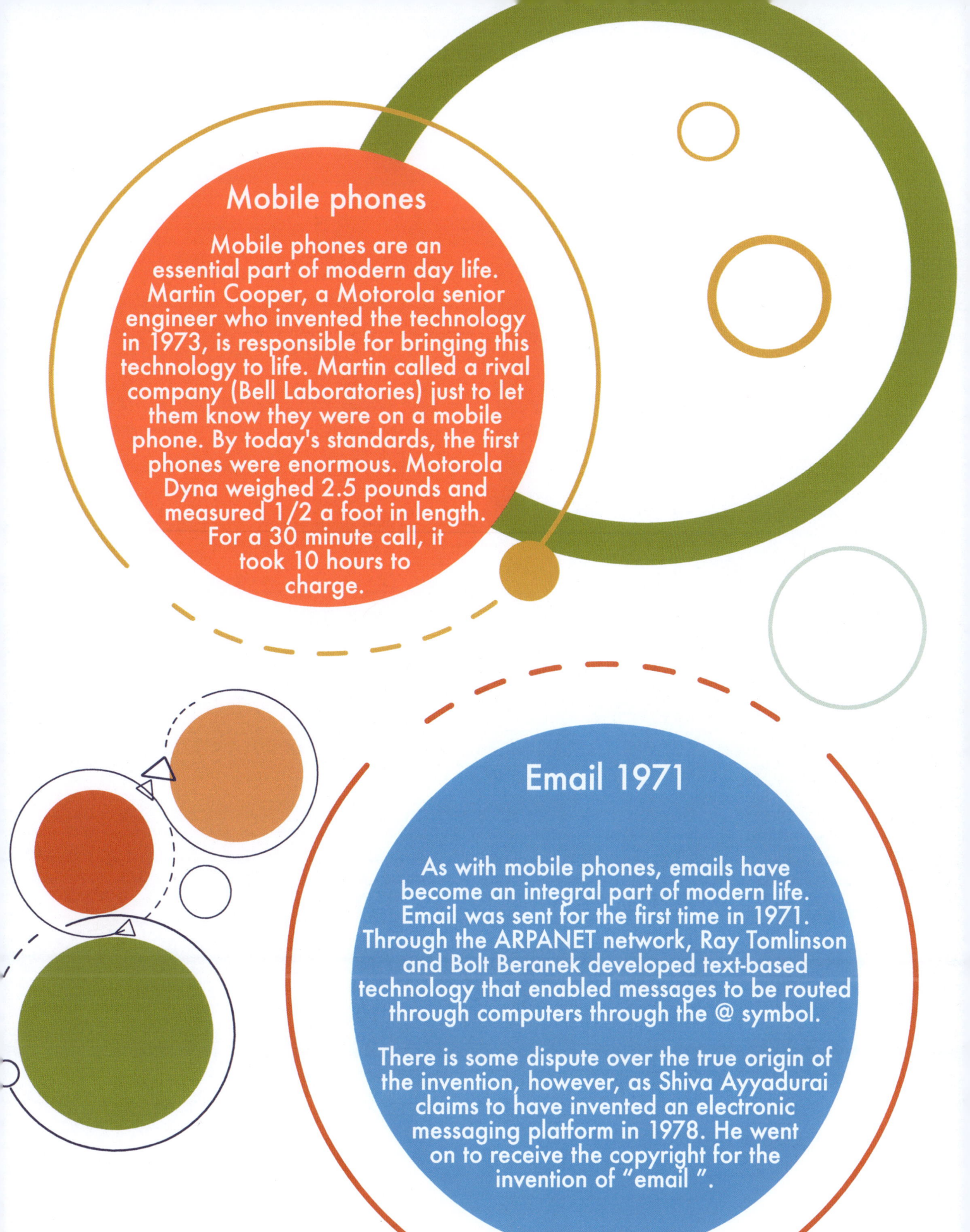

Mobile phones are an essential part of modern day life. Martin Cooper, a Motorola senior engineer who invented the technology in 1973, is responsible for bringing this technology to life. Martin called a rival company (Bell Laboratories) just to let them know they were on a mobile phone. By today's standards, the first phones were enormous. Motorola Dyna weighed 2.5 pounds and measured 1/2 a foot in length. For a 30 minute call, it took 10 hours to charge.

Email 1971

As with mobile phones, emails have become an integral part of modern life. Email was sent for the first time in 1971. Through the ARPANET network, Ray Tomlinson and Bolt Beranek developed text-based technology that enabled messages to be routed through computers through the @ symbol.

There is some dispute over the true origin of the invention, however, as Shiva Ayyadurai claims to have invented an electronic messaging platform in 1978. He went on to receive the copyright for the invention of "email".

Britain in the 70s

It is widely reported that the 1970s were a time of hardship for many due to a struggling economy, strikes, the winter of discontent and general uncertainty that led to social and economic unrest. This decade was marked by constant strikes, primarily by postal workers, miners, and dustmen. In order to reduce electricity consumption, a three-day work week was imposed. To alleviate the shortages caused by the 1973-74 oil crisis, the Conservative government introduced this legislation. Electricity usage for commercial purposes was capped at 3 consecutive days on 1st January 1974, except for hospitals and supermarkets that were exempted. As inflation increased, wages did not rise in line with inflation costs, causing unions to suffer.

Throughout Britain, the Queen's Silver Jubilee was celebrated in 1977. Street parties were held across the nation to celebrate. During this time, many young people were growing dissatisfied with the legitimacy of the monarchy. In 1977, the Sex Pistols released the song 'God Save the Queen' to coincide with the Queen's silver jubilee. A rejection of the monarchy is evident in this song, which reflects the frustration with limited opportunities among young people.

Electing Margaret Thatcher as our first female Prime Minister made history. Despite the bleak picture this paints, and despite the fact that many people vividly recall the power cuts and scarcity of resources, the most shared memories are of happy childhoods, an ease of life that seems far from our technology-crazed world of today. It may just be nostalgia with some rose-tinted glasses thrown in for good measure. Childhood memories of Bagpuss, spacehoppers, and playing with your friends all day tell a story of an idyllic time. Despite the headlines, most ordinary families were doing better than ever.

Food for thought

Only Cannon can give you all this

Eye level open roasting spit—for the tenderest, most succulent meat, poultry and game you have ever tasted. Only on an open spit do you get the Sealed-in Meat juices which make the flavour of the meat so good. It is, literally, done to a turn.

Kebab cooking—dining on a dagger for the family. Go mad with these. Serve Shishkebabs or Shashliks. Dazzle your dinner-guests.

Extra large grill (the only one that folds away) is at eye level—no other grill gives as much visibility—deep as well as wide—see what is cooking from across the room.

Big, automatic oven. Set it, forget it, go away and leave it; it'll cook a whole meal while you're out.

Big feature—enough space for a 25lb turkey. Oven roof slides out for easy cleaning.

Two fast, FAST burners. To keep fried food crisp and green vegetables green, the faster you cook them the better. Two simmering burners for the steady gentle heat you need for a fondue or egg-thickened sauce.

All the refinements: Foldaway grill (4)" back to front when closed; roll out storage drawer; oven light; gas that lights from automatic pilots on the hotplate and in the oven, double-glazed, mist-proof window in oven door. See it at your Gas Appliance Showroom. Under the model number Cannon 133 RD.

Cannon
sturdy, spacious, civilised.

The legal stuff...

All rights reserved @ Little Pips Press

2024

Attribution for photo images goes to the following talented photographers under the creative commons licenses specified:

Attribution 4.0 International (CC BY 4.0)
Attribution-ShareAlike 4.0 International (CC BY-SA 4.0)
Attribution 2.0 Generic (CC BY 2.0)
Attribution-ShareAlike 2.0 Generic (CC BY-SA 2.0)

https://www.flickr.com/photos/ausdew/36262420464/in/faves-189870699@N02
https://www.flickr.com/photos/dannybirchall/6371775259/in/faves-189870699@N02
https://www.flickr.com/photos/newcastlelibraries/4080882808/in/faves-189870699@N02/
https://www.flickr.com/photos/andrea_44/2518095430/in/gallery-189870699@N02-72157717773240902/
https://www.flickr.com/photos/27718315@N02/10853507566/in/gallery-189870699@N02-72157717773240902/
https://www.flickr.com/photos/stuart166axe/2961407449/in/gallery-189870699@N02-72157717773240902/
https://www.flickr.com/photos/daveparker/33810231/in/gallery-189870699@N02-72157717773240902/
https://www.flickr.com/photos/preetamrai/5283158/in/gallery-189870699@N02-72157717773240902/
https://www.flickr.com/photos/chellebella/124257384/in/gallery-189870699@N02-72157717773240902/
https://www.flickr.com/photos/jdxyw/4845074729/in/gallery-189870699@N02-72157717773240902/
https://www.flickr.com/photos/badgreeb_records/6432940755/in/gallery-189870699@N02-72157717773240902/
https://www.flickr.com/photos/51764518@N02/25906691193/in/gallery-189870699@N02-72157717773240902/
https://www.flickr.com/photos/acemegarex/50032561523/in/gallery-189870699@N02-72157717773240902/
https://www.flickr.com/photos/xlbrett/50573390891/in/gallery-189870699@N02-72157717773240902/
https://www.flickr.com/photos/7thstreettheatre/46844185454/in/gallery-189870699@N02-72157717773240902/
https://www.flickr.com/photos/89375753@N00/50207925792/in/gallery-189870699@N02-72157717773240902/
https://www.flickr.com/photos/ateam/4239144680/in/gallery-189870699@N02-72157717773240902/
https://www.flickr.com/photos/8724914@N08/46687874422/in/gallery-189870699@N02-72157717773240902/
https://www.flickr.com/photos/nick99nack/24091207203/in/gallery-189870699@N02-72157717773240902/
https://www.flickr.com/photos/romitagirl67/23523223366/in/gallery-189870699@N02-72157717773240902/

https://www.flickr.com/photos/deanoakley/4554150774/in/gallery-189870699@N02-72157717773240902/
https://www.flickr.com/photos/84369496@N00/840793424/in/gallery-189870699@N02-72157717773240902/
https://www.flickr.com/photos/vintage19something/6051561814/in/gallery-189870699@N02-72157717773240902/
https://www.flickr.com/photos/148686664@N06/45511988572/in/gallery-189870699@N02-72157717773240902/
https://www.flickr.com/photos/lizjones/1812995239/in/faves-189870699@N02
https://www.flickr.com/photos/jurvetson/75152484118/in/faves-189870699@N02
https://www.flickr.com/photos/currybet/3433417635/in/faves-189870699@N02
https://www.flickr.com/photos/robinparker/5985075605/in/faves-189870699@N02
https://www.flickr.com/photos/londonmatt/31871854060/in/faves-189870699@N02
https://www.flickr.com/photos/jonevans/302797355/in/faves-189870699@N02
https://www.flickr.com/photos/15979685@N08/50851583163/in/faves-189870699@N02/
https://www.flickr.com/photos/westmidlandspolice/13557849404/in/faves-189870699@N02/
https://www.flickr.com/photos/xlbrett/7948090712/in/faves-189870699@N02
https://www.flickr.com/photos/33657268@N04/5352666481/in/faves-189870699@N02/
https://www.flickr.com/photos/56832361@N00/347414491/in/faves-189870699@N02
https://www.flickr.com/photos/lisa_yarost/552931318/in/faves-189870699@N02
https://www.flickr.com/photos/ausdew/36262420464/in/faves-189870699@N02
https://www.flickr.com/photos/antmcneill/5963414170/in/faves-189870699@N02
https://www.flickr.com/photos/newcastlelibraries/4080882808/in/faves-189870699@N02/
https://www.flickr.com/photos/dannybirchall/6371775259/in/faves-189870699@N02
https://www.flickr.com/photos/jodiepedia/27611238548/in/faves-189870699@N02
https://www.flickr.com/photos/rhian/8867801538/in/faves-189870699@N02/
https://www.flickr.com/photos/autohistorian/27642890463/in/faves-189870699@N02
https://www.flickr.com/photos/juanelo242a/38087131886/in/faves-189870699@N02
https://www.flickr.com/photos/hugo90/25884537906/in/faves-189870699@N02/
https://www.flickr.com/photos/123723459@N07/27085005701/in/faves-189870699@N02/
https://www.flickr.com/photos/123723459@N07/27085005701/in/faves-189870699@N02/
https://www.flickr.com/photos/garlandcannon/28367018924/in/faves-189870699@N02/
https://www.flickr.com/photos/richardsummers/2392407529/in/faves-189870699@N02/
https://www.flickr.com/photos/jdxyw/4845074729/in/faves-189870699@N02

Printed in Great Britain
by Amazon